Real Men Don't Play

A Journey of Manhood

Edward N. Jackson

ROYSTON
Publishing

BK Royston Publishing
Jeffersonville, IN
bkroystonpublishing@gmail.com

© Copyright 2024

All Rights Reserved. No part of this book may be reproduced, stored in a retrieval system, or transmitted by any means without the written permission of the author.

Cover Design: Elite Book Covers
Author Photography: Elder Josif Kates

ISBN-13: 978-1-963136-02-9

Printed in the United States of America

Dedication

This book is proudly dedicated to my wife, Carolyn, of 45 years of marriage, who has since gone on to be with the Lord, but was a world traveler in and out of cities and airports throughout the United States, Kuwait, and the Middle East, supporting me through the years of our family needs in today's changing world. To my two loving and caring daughters, Kimberly (Kim) and Cynthia (Cindy), both of whom have allowed me to be Mr. Mom while their mother busied herself, making a career that today they now cherish as mothers themselves. I thank God for two wonderful daughters who gave their parents the most wonderful grandchildren a grandfather and grandmother could ever hope for.

Last but not least, my sincere gratitude is extended to my friend and mentor, Dr. Stewart Reese Jr., who, like Christ, always tries to find the good in the worst situation.

Acknowledgements

I want to express my deepest, heartfelt thanks to:

Dr. and Mrs. Stewart Reese Jr. helped me realize through life's problems that you can be faithful and true to God, your wife, and family. Also, I'm thankful for the many conversations and times Dr. Reese would share his wealth of knowledge and experiences to enlighten and bless others like me.

The team of the Atlanta radio talk show Men Let's Talk at www.love860.com (WAEC 860AM, at 6:45 pm until 7:15 pm, Mondays), especially Terrell Johnson, Kevin Vaughan, Dr. Torri Griffin, and our many affiliates for their assistance in allowing the Lord to work in our entire radio endeavor. Thanks for the team's willingness to help me compile and arrange my research, as well as communicate my thoughts. Their scholarly edge keeps me asking the right questions and seeking God for the right answers.

Thanks also go to my Spanish partners, especially Amanda Crump, and my Lockheed Martin coworkers, especially Annette Moore, for the wonderfully gracious way they would tolerate my minefield of thoughts, questions, and answers.

Most of all, I thank God for my parents, God rest their souls, who knew someday their country-born Nashville boy would make good of the name they gave him at birth, "Neriah" (The Light of God). For the many friends throughout my life who made me realize Jesus is the best thing that we could ever have in life.

Last but not least, all the great men of God whom I have had the privilege of sitting under, who have taught me from God's Word that "Greater is "HE" that is in me than "he" that is in the world."

Table of Contents

Dedication	iii
Acknowledgment	v
Foreword	ix
Introduction	xiii
Chapter One: The Making of a Man	1
Chapter Two: When a Man Finds a Wife	17
Chapter Three: When a Man Becomes a Father	33
Chapter Four: Real Men Don't Play When the Wife's Away	45

Chapter Five: *63*
What God will do when a
Man is Faithful

About the Author   *75*

Foreword

by
Dr. Torri Griffin, LPC

Real men don't play when the wives are away. Real men don't play—period. Boys play, and adolescents play. They play ball, they play games…they even play house. But real men know the value of putting away childish things and being responsible adults in their lives and relationships. Real men who marry know the value of their word when spoken in the vows… "To love, honor, and cherish, from this day forward, till death do us part." Real men choose to love even when no one is looking. Real men choose to honor and cherish even when they are talking to an attractive, single woman in a private setting. Real men know that this day will be followed by many days in which they and their beloved will be apart and may find themselves away from each other for weeks or months at a time. Real men know that marriage is a commitment—a commitment for life.

Statistics show that many males are walking down the aisles in search of wedded bliss. Statistics also show that many married males are ill-equipped to manage their homes, families, and even themselves when tough times come. Marriage is a job for real men who understand the preparation it takes to properly lead the family. Preparation is the key ingredient in preparing the mix of spiritual, emotional, social, financial, and sexual responsibility.

Real Men Don't Play When the Wife's Away looks at the challenges that men face in becoming men, seeking wives, becoming parents, serving God, and being accountable. It takes special diligence to accomplish each step adequately enough to provide the foundation to withstand the desire and the lure to play when the wife's away.

The allure is caused by statistics that say there are far more available women than men in certain communities. The allure is caused by many who disdain marriage and the marriage commitment that upholds monogamy as its standard. The allure is also caused by the misinformation that an affair requires sexual intimacy and omits emotional intimacy.

While many of today's men pride themselves on being 'playa's' and having their women on a tier system of importance in their lives, real men know the value of creating the image God intended for them in marriage.

Marriage is a mystery, just as the message of a loving Heavenly Father sending his Son to the earth to reconcile all people back to Him is a mystery. Marriage is the most significant and sacred of all covenants, and it is because it is most representative of God's covenant with the world. It is love personified. It is God's visual example of how He feels about us. Jesus is to His church as the husband is to be to his wife—loving her at his own expense as he develops and secures her in his love.

If you intend to be a real man in marriage or if you are involved with a real man in marriage, you know that this man's love for his wife is solid regardless of whether she is one foot or one continent away. This love is shown in tangible and intangible ways, allowing her and other women to feel secure in his company. When a real man is around, other women know he's happily married and unavailable for a short-term, brief encounter that will do irreparable damage to them all.

His commitment shows in all he does, including his commitment to wearing his wedding ring. So many men these days are willing to send mixed messages to women that open them up to flirtatious and suggestive invitations. Simply standing as a real man in all settings creates an atmosphere of security and confidence that anyone around can stand on. What the world needs now is more real men who don't play when their wives are away.

Introduction

"But seek ye first the kingdom of God, and his righteousness; and all these things shall be added unto you."
Matthews 6:33 (KJV)

      I was living in Wichita, Kansas, during the 1980s when a well-known pastor was requested to carry on a much-needed revival. The revival was needed because I was the one seeking and needing direction from the Lord. I had been praying and fasting that the Lord would make me successful. I wanted the Lord to make me successful in my chosen career as an engineer. I wanted Him to make me successful as a husband to my wife and father to my daughters. Successful in ministry. The preacher during that revival anointed me one night with olive oil and prayed over my life. I walked away from that week-long revival, knowing that my life would be different from that moment on. Something happened that reassured me that the Lord was truly concerned about what was going on in my life. So, I decided to read the Word of God and revisit the rules, commandments, and laws that would help a young man in his quest to be successful. And guess what I found was the first law of being successful, right here and right now? It's setting the right goal! Set the right goal!

Jesus clearly established the highest-priority goal for his disciples in Matthew 6:33. While Jesus established this priority, He also knew that this main goal, our highest priority, determines the amount of preparation, effort, and zeal for reaching all other goals in this present world.

For example, suppose someone who only spoke the American language offered us a tremendous sum of money, perhaps billions of dollars. But the exact amount would be determined by how well we could learn to speak Spanish in two months. We would perhaps embark on the most intense crash-course learning program in our lives! We would study from morning to night, burn the midnight oil, listen to language tapes, carry flashcards wherever we went, and seek out fluent Spanish speakers to practice with them.

During those two months, no one could drag us near a time-wasting television program. If we watched any TV at all, it would be in Spanish. We would probably allow nothing to interfere with our learning other than the necessary physical activities to sustain life, all for our share of that money! Notice what Jesus says earlier in Matthew chapter 6.

"Do not lay up for yourselves treasures on earth, where moth and rust destroy and where thieves break in and steal; but lay up for yourselves treasures in heaven, where neither moth nor rust destroys and where thieves do not break in and steal. For where your treasure is, there your heart will be also" Matthew 6:19-21(KJV).

Consider these scriptures in the context of what Jesus says in verse 33. Our hearts are in the things to which we devote ourselves and spend our time pursuing. The Lord is helping us prioritize our lives by stating and illustrating principles that will help us make the right choices in managing time and all other resources we have to utilize.

Every day, another 24 hours, some 1,440 minutes, or 86,400 seconds, is credited to our account, and we must spend them. Whether we are Wall Street billionaires or dirt farmers in Kansas, all of us have the same amount of time accounted to us every morning the Lord gives us life. Jesus already knows how we spend our time and shows where our heart is.

Of course, Bible study and prayer are very high-priority activities in seeking the Kingdom of God. But Satan also knows this! Satan knows it would be difficult to change our minds regarding their value if he confronted us directly. So, he uses subtle, indirect approaches to confuse us, and all too often, he succeeds in diverting our attention from these high-priority concerns.

Subsequently, at the end of each chapter, you'll find a section entitled "Principles of Manhood." This section is designed to help get the most from a chapter by studying and/or joining others in a group or workshop to work through the questions presented in the chapters. So, for example, let's deal with what has been established in the "Introduction" of this book.

"Principles of Manhood"

1. *What is the first law that our Lord and Savior set for his disciples according to Matthew 6:33? Why?*

   _____

   _____

   _____

2. *What other scriptures can you find to support this prioritizing law our Lord establishes in Matthew chapter 6:33?*

   _____

   _____

   _____

3. *How would you learn when the reward(s) demand your best efforts in the shortest period?*

   _____

   _____

   _____

4. *What kind of things are you presently devoting your heart to accomplish?*

   _____

   _____

   _____

5. *God's Word challenges each of us to attend a Bible study this week and ask the teacher or facilitator one question that will help us focus on the goals we should set for our lives.*

6. *Well, do you get the idea? Let's study to show ourselves approved by the Word of God.*

Chapter One

"When I was a child, I spake as a child, I understood as a child, I thought as a child: but when I became a man, I put away childish things."
1 Corinthians 13:11 (KJV)

The Making of a Man

Human and holy. Can a man truly be both? In many ways, being human and being holy is a contradiction in terms. But that is the challenge every man faces daily in our walk with the Lord. It's no different for our wives and children; they are also challenged by an enemy that cares nothing about the love of God dwelling in our lives. As men of God, we were made to be holy, to be set apart, sanctified, and saved by the blood of Jesus Christ. As human beings, however, we must confess a not-so-flattering truth: we are not holy. We men are sinners called to be saints. Our situation is like trying to drive a bent nail into concrete. The tools we think we should use are inadequate for the task. The only real tool that could ever shape any man was, is, and will be the Word of God.

From the beginning of time, the Lord God knew precisely what he wanted a man to be. When God created Adam, he said, **"Let us make man in our image, after our likeness…So God created man in his image, in the image of God created him" Genesis 1:26, 27 (KJV).** God's Word shaped man then, and it is still His Word that will mold and make boys into men. There is something inside every man that longs to be like Christ, but we wrestle in our minds, with our bodies, the thoughts that come to overtake our being a human wrapped in flesh.

Every man seeking to be Christ-like should have at least one other man who is also striving to be like Christ as an accountability partner while going through life. Having an accountability partner is a must in our present society. Now, having an accountability partner is not a guarantee that there will always be open and honest dialog between partners, but having an accountability partner gives you the opportunity to share your genuine emotions and feelings with someone as trials and problems come your way.

So many married men and bachelors in our present society are losing the battle with lust and are quickly falling into fornication and adultery. But striving for Christlikeness and having an accountability partner who will share and intercede in prayers will and can help each of us through these pits that have claimed so many men. So, when a man realizes that he cannot live without the intimate relationship of a woman, then he must ask himself what so many other men, throughout time and history, have had to come to grips with.

Can a man be complete without that remarkable woman, his companion, his wife? Genesis 2:18 records, **"And the LORD God said, It is not good that the man should be alone; I will make him an help meet for him."**

Paul said in **1 Corinthian 7:1-2 KJV,** **"Now concerning the things whereof ye wrote unto me: It is good for a man not to touch a woman. Nevertheless, to avoid fornication, let every man have his own wife, and let every woman have her own husband."**

Most men, as they go through their bachelorhood, have sought and are looking for the affection and love of women. But there are those men, according to psychologists, who have not cared to get married for other reasons. Most psychologists agree that men fall into four different areas.

A large number of men rejecting marriage are fixated on a mother figure. These men live at home with their mothers until the death of the parent "releases" them, and then these men find it challenging to carve out a different kind of life with a woman in marriage. The mother figure that dominated their lives continues to dominate the image of what they seek in a woman as their partner in marriage.

A second and familiar type is the man who is not so much antinomian, believing that under the gospel dispensation of grace, the moral law is useless as anti-responsible. Panicking at the thought of heading a household, he spends a lifetime evading marriage while believing he is seeking it. These unmarried men carry a heavy psychological burden of being the head of a household. These men are raised with admonitions to "be a man and be independent," some become confused over the conflict between their determination to be truly self-reliant and the need to lean on a woman for love and comfort.

A third troubled group consists of latent homosexuals. These fall into two classes—the "neuter," who practices no sexual activity of any kind and is often found working in boys' schools and boys' organizations, and the "Don Juan," who is so threatened by his fears of his unacknowledged homosexuality that he engages in affairs with women to prove his masculinity.

The fourth group consists of confirmed homosexuals who are becoming more visible, with notable numbers that seem to continue to rise.

While emotional problems are common among single men, several unwed men adjust completely to life without women and find a thoroughly satisfying existence alone. Some of these men seem to have found fulfillment in their working lives exclusively. Examples can be found in every field. Other men find a sense of completion by rounding out their business lives with an engrossing hobby, often in sports.

However well he may adjust to his lonely life, the single man suffers disabilities that seem to be traceable directly to his bachelorhood. Unwed men are much less healthy than their married brothers. A Metropolitan Life Insurance Company study reflects that more than four times as many unattached men as married men (ages 20–74) die of tuberculosis. At ages 20–44, five to six times as many unmarried men die of influenza and pneumonia as husbands. Before mid-life, nine divorced men had cirrhosis of the liver compared to each married man killed by that disease.

These studies indicate that of all the men without women, the divorced are in the worst physical condition. Widowers ranked second in physical suffering, and bachelors were third.

Away from the sick bed, the lives of the unwed are still hazardous. Widowers and divorced men (20–44) are four times as likely to be killed in automobile accidents as husbands. Five divorced men commit suicide to each married man. In homicide, the picture is even darker. Out of every 100,000 men (20–74) in this country, 24 divorced men are murdered, as are 17 widowers and eight bachelors—while only four married men die at the hands of a killer.

"Of all interpersonal relationships in our society, marriage is at the same time the most rewarding and most demanding." Unmarried men believe that should be encouraged by the one point almost all authorities agree on: if you really want to get married, it is never too late.

So, I don't find it strange when a man looks over his shoulder and makes gestures or whistles when he sees a woman that he finds attractive. From the beginning of time, every woman has had that God-giving ability to catch the eyes of a man and make him do some mighty, strange things in trying to win her heart and hand in marriage. In the maturing and making of a man, some strange and immature things do happen.

What I also find strange is the complacent attitude of men who accept the teachings of learned and anointed men of God who have committed their lives and taken their precious time to live, understand, and know God's Word. Men who have taken the time to understand how much better life has been and will be if we trust in the truths of the Word of God. His Word gives all men truths and understandings that have been blessings handed down and passed on from God to men, from fathers to sons, since the beginning of time. Why do we continue to kick against the pricks and bang our heads against the walls? Let's not take the Word of God for granted anymore. Let's read it. Let's understand the rewards that flow from understanding God's Word and the men who have taught, lived, and believed in it. God's Word is majestic and powerful, and the men who trust in God are mighty.

The majestic Word of God motivates me to teach its truths. So, when I step into the auditoriums of cathedrals and churches to find small groups of men barely hanging on to the majestic promises and stories of the Word of God, I'm once again motivated to teach. Some churches with their membership rolls reflecting hundreds of men, with just a few good men, in a small room hanging on to the promises of God.

So, when I see men ignoring the Word of God and anointed men of God, I don't find it strange to see the divorce rate soaring higher and higher. I don't find it odd that in our world today, we have such a growing number of homosexual unions. The institution of marriage is suffering because we once again are ignoring the teaching and preaching of God's Word. We will continue to see married men running after women in extramarital affairs when there is no Word of God in one's life. We clearly see that when the Word of

God is removed from the understanding of a man's heart, he will engage himself in an intimate relationship outside the bonds of marriage, time and time again. Now, I'm not saying that it's easy to look the other way when that handsome, already-married man or that sexually willing and beautiful lady is talking and looking like the perfect love of your life. What I am saying is that the Almighty Father has entrusted each man and woman to be faithful and chase to Him until they are married, and this same trust and faithfulness will keep you throughout your marriage. Forsaking all others until death, do you part. Real men trust God to be the Lord of their lives and to abide by the commandments of a loving God that keeps you and blesses you through good times and bad times, too.

You see, faith is trust in God. Not just any kind of trust; it's obedient trust in the Lord and not just any type of obedient trust. Faith is radical obedience and trust in the Lord. When a man develops radical obedience and trust to believe what God says, God will bless that man despite what others say. That's it. That's how a man is made. God will make you a man of men when he puts his faith entirely in "Him."

Principles of Manhood

Chapter Two

"Therefore, shall a man leave his father and his mother, and shall cleave unto his wife: and they shall be one flesh."
Genesis 2:24 (KJV)

When a Man Finds a Wife

There's a great responsibility in becoming a Husband. Each man must decide to be responsible not only for his life but for the lives of others. A committed man of God is a law-abiding citizen, working through his day-to-day problems. Working through his issues will determine how greatly he will accept his responsibilities. You must ask yourself. Am I self-reliant and dependable? Can others trust me to be there through thick and thin? When a man accepts his responsibilities in life, he is then ready for the responsibility of being a faithful man to one woman and being faithful to that one woman for the rest of his life.

Guys, the odds are stacked against women who long for a stable home and family. The pool of worthwhile, responsible, marriageable men is drying up. The rise of homosexuality has cut into that number. The increase in crime has taken a much bigger bite. In the black community, there are more men in prison than there are in college. In some parts of the country, the ratio of men to women is shrinking to the point where there are five women for each man. But how many men are willing to commit to Christ and step up to their responsibilities in life? A committed Christian woman is looking for a man who will fulfill his role as the spiritual head of the household.

The Word of God says, "Whosoever findeth a wife findeth a good thing, and obtaineth favour of the Lord." Proverbs 18:22 (KJV)

The wisdom of King Solomon in Proverb 31:10-31 (KJV) records the true beauty of what you have in a committed Christian woman.

The man who selects his bride, according to Proverbs 31, is no fool. So many men base their decisions on secular criteria and, too often, find that they got less than what they bargained for.

Men, the choice is yours. You can base your selection on what you see at the movies or what you read in the Bible, God's word. The screens of our theaters and television sets are filled with lovely ladies. But that kind of physical attractiveness goes no deeper than the two-dimensional image that flickers in front of us. We live in a day when many things, especially cosmetics, can turn practically any woman into a beauty queen. We live in a day when 14-year-old girls can be made to look like 25-year-old women. We live in a day when beauty has become a false criterion for what men value.

Of course, beauty has its place. However, heed the warning of Solomon:

"Beauty is vain" Proverbs 31:30 (KJV).

Remember, beauty has an unbeatable enemy, "time." Inevitably, wrinkles, weight, grey hair, cellulite, and gravity have their way of repainting your picture of loveliness.

Guys, we are not talking about ordinary females. Solomon is referring to a class of women who rise above the crowd. Such women need not be concerned about male/female ratios. They are "special, noble women of great and impeccable dignity." These ladies would never associate themselves with men who rub diamonds in the dirt. These committed Christian ladies ask the Lord for a God-fearing man who can handle precious stones.

So, you've looked high and low for that special lady, to no avail. But have you obtained the favor of the Father? Have you taken the time to be faithful and trustworthy in your daily walk with the Lord? Have you asked the Father for her hand and heart? When you decide to talk to the Father, I guarantee the Lord knows if you qualify for one of his daughters. When you find favor with the Father, you have found the path to her heart, for God processes and cherishes the hearts of his daughters.

I mentioned earlier that the rise of homosexuality is pulling from the pool of marriageable men. For just a few minutes, let me address the truth of men becoming lovers and homosexual unions. There is a growing awareness of more men than ever before becoming infatuated with the thoughts of being in love and wanting to be in a union with another man. First, let me say that I care for all men, and my prayers are that every man's heart burns for the love of a woman. There is no substitute for the love of a God-given woman, absolutely none. Every man ought to know that if his desires for an intimate relationship are not found in a woman, then something is wrong with his relationship with God. Homosexuality has been around for a long time, and I'm persuaded that homosexuals will be around until the end of this world. The Word of

God, as it is recorded in II Timothy 3:1-2 (KJV) says:

"This know also, that in the last days perilous times shall come. For men shall be lovers of their own selves..."

I have seen and been with some of the most gifted, brilliant, and incredible men who have allowed themselves to be tricked by the enemy with this idea that you can love and be in a union with another man. Evil men and seducers are trying to sexually corrupt as many children, young boys and girls, teenagers, and young adults as they can. Once the minds and lives of our youth have been violated by corruption, we can never restore their innocence. We can never restore the loving innocence of children who once walked the halls of schools, violated by teachers with little or no morals. Courtrooms that once stood for law and justice are now compromised by a weakening moral decay that removes the commandments of God. But the Word of God can make us wise so that the man of God may be perfected and matured.

The absence of a wife in a marriage relationship cannot yield life. But the making of a man, a real man, is when he grows up to understand that God wants him to be with one woman as one flesh. When a man and his God-given woman, his wife, come together as one, there is life. God is the life-giver, and a man with another man cannot yield life. It's that simple. God is life, and without God in your life, there is no life. Listen to what Apostle Paul had to say about leaving the natural affection of a woman, as recorded in Romans 1:27-32 (KJV).

"And likewise also the men, leaving the natural use of the woman, burned in their lust one toward another; men with men working that which is unseemly, and receiving in themselves that recompense of their error which was meet. And even as they did not like to retain God in their knowledge, God gave them over to a reprobate mind, to do those things which are not convenient; Being filled with all unrighteousness, fornication, wickedness, covetousness, maliciousness; full of envy, murder, debate, deceit, malignity; whisperers, Backbiters, haters of God, despiteful, proud, boasters, inventors of evil things, disobedient to parents,

Without understanding, covenant breakers, without natural affection, implacable, unmerciful: Who knowing

the judgment of God, that they which commit such things are worthy of death, not only do the same but have pleasure in them that do them."

Carolyn and I celebrated our thirtieth wedding anniversary on August 1, 2005. Our thirtieth wedding anniversary truly was different. I sat in a restaurant enjoying my anniversary dinner at Copeland in Kennesaw, a few miles from Atlanta, Georgia, and Carolyn in Kuwait City, Kuwait. Carolyn had e-mailed me earlier that week and asked me just to remember her while I enjoyed a nice dinner. I sat there at the dinner table thinking over and over, again and again, how the years had passed and how good God had been through the good times and hard times. I thought about how many of our dreams and desires were fulfilled even as I sat at that dinner table. Carolyn is now working in countries where we could only dream about visiting, seeing, and talking to people we could only read about in books. It makes me feel good knowing that her desires and career have gone so well.

Paul says, "The woman is the glory of the man." Every man who loves God and is married is on assignment from God to help his wife become his glory! So, what can a husband do so God can grow in a wife's heart committed to helping her husband and yet fulfill her God-given assignment?

Consider these suggestions:

1. Make a commitment to help your wife—The decision to serve is yours. No one can decide for you, and no one can force you to decide. You must make the decision as a husband who loves God.

You want to encourage her as she seeks her career goals and desires.

2. Focus a little more on your wife–God wants husbands to focus a lot more of their energies and efforts on their wives–her tasks, goals, and responsibilities. But beware, our fleshly nature will cry out selfishly, "Me first." But God wants us to say to our wives, "You first." Just like when you politely escorted her through the doors of your favorite restaurant.

3. Question your actions: will this help or hinder my wife? By asking this simple question of ourselves before we act, we have a better chance of choosing the right conduct that will help our wives build trust and confidence in their husbands.

4. Helping. Being a gentleman. It's a simple yet noble assignment–one that will give you high rewards. Not only will our wives benefit, but we will, too and learn to serve as Christ did for the church.

When a man and his wife come together as one in the Lord, they begin a faith journey, each of them maturing and getting to know each other through their day-to-day life challenges. He is not complete without her, and she is not complete without him. He and she are complete in marriage. Marriage is about "love." God is "love." The God of "love" is making him more mindful of his need to be a loving and trustworthy husband and a loving and trustworthy wife. In this bond of marriage, everything is built on trust. She is trusting in him, and he is trusting in her, and both are trusting in the Lord.

Principles of Manhood

Chapter Three

"Come, my children, listen to me; I will teach you the fear of the Lord."
Psalm 34:11 (KJV)

When a Man Becomes a Father

God views the addition of children to a family as a great gift. In Psalm 127:3-5, the psalmist wrote, **"Lo, children are an heritage of the Lord: and the fruit of the womb is his reward. As arrows are in the hand of a mighty man, so are the children of the youth. Happy is the man that hath his quiver full of them: they shall not be ashamed, but they shall speak with the enemies in the gates."**

When God blesses a man to have children, serious responsibilities fall upon his shoulders. But with the God-ordained marriage that is blessed with children, there are added responsibilities that fall upon the shoulders of the parents. These added responsibilities are not a burden; they are simply part of God's plan for their maturity in Him.

When a man becomes a father, now he must provide not only for his wife but for his children as well. He must pass on to his children the lessons and skills that life has unfolded for him, with the knowledge of knowing that God was, is, and will continue to be the source and strength for his children. In 1 Timothy 5:8, Paul wrote, **"But if any provide not for his own, and especially for those of his own house, he hath denied the faith, and is worse than an infidel."** A father must provide them with food, clothing, shelter, and all the other physical things necessary for their well-being.

However, a father owes his children much more than the physical necessities. He owes his children other necessary things that are more important than the physical, and they are things that money cannot buy. A father owes his children leadership, guidance, and a good example. His children must be able to look to him for advice and counsel. Remember, in Ephesians 6:4, the Bible says, **"And, ye fathers, provoke not your children to wrath: but bring them up in the nurture and admonition of the Lord."** Much is involved in that statement. Many men feel that since they go out and earn a living, the rest of the responsibility for the children rests with the mother. That is not the case in the God-ordained home. While she shares the responsibility of teaching the children, God puts the first duty on the father as the head of the household to bring his children up in the "nurture and admonition of the Lord."

To be an example, to be the guiding influence that a father is to be, there must be time spent with the children. So many fathers, either because of work or social activities (clubs and associations), spend very little time with their children. We certainly would not be pleased with a schoolteacher who didn't spend the necessary time with the children. We would feel that that individual was not doing the job. Well, God places the primary responsibility for the children's "education" upon the father. As one who has spent many years in Sunday Schools teaching God's children of all ages, I can tell you that the happiest, most well-adjusted kids were those whose parents spent time with them. The father who always has something else to do instead of spending time with his children is just too busy. All the money in the world cannot do for the children what a father's presence and interest in their lives can do.

In addition, there is the matter of discipline. So often, when discipline is mentioned, the immediate thought is punishment of some form or another. That is just a part of discipline, not all of it. Solomon wrote in Proverbs 22:6, **"Train up a child in the way he should go: and when he is old, he will not depart from it."** Discipline, when used as a noun, means "training which corrects, molds, strengthens, or perfects." When it is used as a verb, it means "to develop by instruction and exercise, to train in self-control and obedience." It can also mean "to punish, to chastise." A father's responsibility is to set certain guidelines for his children to follow and then discipline them to follow them. This way, the children learn respect for authority, self-control, and restraint. Occasionally, corporeal punishment will be necessary. In Proverb 13:24, the Bible says, **"He that spareth his rod hateth his son;**

but he that loveth him chasteneth him betimes." This is a responsibility that is assumed when a man becomes a father.

Fathers, our children need us much more than they need things, and God expects us to supply that need. Becoming a father and a parent can be a most rewarding yet challenging effort.

Now, fathers, your children will challenge you to fulfill your God-ordained role, and as a role model, you are to be mature and wise as you strive to keep your children under control. Furthermore, never provoke your children to argue, fuss, or fight. What a challenge! But a father is to bring his children up under the discipline and instruction of the Lord. Ephesians 6:3, 4 says, **"Make every effort to keep the unity of the Spirit through the bond of peace. There is one body and one Spirit**

- just as you were called to one hope when you were called."

Remember, train up a child in the way they should go; even when they are older, they will not depart from what you have taught and modeled. If a man is married and has children, he should have a well-managed and well-ordered household.

Remember, children can be a challenge, but with patience and faith, each child will grow to love and cherish the love and the trust that you birth into their lives with each crisis or problem that may enter their lives. We, husbands, should live with our wives in an atmosphere of listening, understanding, and talking about our problems in such a manner that our children learn to resolve their problems the same way—always focusing on the problem to resolve it and not to damage or hurt one another.

Setting a good example or being a good role model often requires not only ingenuity but also great effort. The minds and hearts of children will more than likely be touched when they see their father really trying. A son or a daughter will remember the times you came home tired from work but took the time to help them with their seemingly little time-consuming happenings. Clearly, setting a good example in both word and deed is vital to being a good father. Remember, it is not only what you say that matters; it is particularly what you do, the example you set. If you want your children to value spiritual matters, it is essential that you do so yourself.

Your children must see your good example. That means you need to spend a lot of time with them. Really, what is more important than your children?

Fathers should be actively involved in teaching their children.

There is a familiar saying, "Pay now, or pay later." Fathers whose children have been lost to immoral activity or even to a lifestyle devoid of spirituality often feel deep remorse. They lament that they failed to be with their little ones more often when they really needed a father.

Principles of Manhood

Chapter Four

"So, he that goeth in to his neighbour's wife; whosoever toucheth her shall not be innocent."
Proverbs 6:29 (KJV)

Real Men Don't Play When the Wife's Away

When the cat's away, the mice will play. Surely, by now, you've heard about this true fact of life. But the real question is, "Are we mice or men"? Throughout history, man has struggled with his fidelity and his infidelities. While we have all struggled, and so many have yielded to sexual temptations, the real cause has been the lack of having a true and real relationship with God.

You see when the cat roams the house, the mice don't venture out in fear of sudden death from the cat's claws. When the cat lurks around the house, the mice are careful to dart and sneak about in hopes that the cat will not catch them. When men don't know God, they sneak about darting here and there, thinking they can get away without being caught. Wrong. God has a way of finding you and letting your wife know your mischievousness, and once she knows, you have a serious problem. Your vulnerability to playing around can cost you your life. We read about men being shot, killed, and divorced every day.

Let me help you to understand the number one reason most men are vulnerable to sexual temptations in their marriage. Men are most vulnerable to sexual temptation in marriage when they are unable to achieve their goals, frustrated, discouraged, or when dreams are being dashed. The sexual involvement grows out of feeling that their lives are out of control, that they are inadequate and weak. When life is not affirming a man's value as a person, he becomes more vulnerable. Then along comes a person who affirms the hurting man's value, who accepts him just as he is, and who indicates she finds him very attractive. And when the hurting man becomes involved, it's a way of proving to himself that someone still wants him and that someone still finds him attractive.

Almost always, this "other woman" is not as attractive physically as the hurting man's spouse, and the main reason is that the infidelity doesn't grow primarily out of physical desires. Still, the wandering husband's ego or self-image is at stake. If a man's dreams and aspirations are continually belittled or taken for granted, the person is going to be more vulnerable to the approach of someone who is supportive.

Middle age often brings with it a particular vulnerability to sexual temptation, too. Some men become afraid of growing older and are tempted to test the waters to find out. Then, there are relationships that are spawned by emotional and intellectual intimacies through social contacts and significant conversations about personal topics. The development of a warm relationship into something with sexual overtones can be very subtle, which makes it all the more dangerous.

Given the usual process by which sexual temptation and sin come about, it naturally follows that the most important part of resisting sexual temptation is to maintain a good marriage relationship. That's the key and the answer. If the marriage relationship meets the needs God intended, a man won't usually look to get those needs met elsewhere. This means a husband and wife must work toward each other's goals. I said work, and I do mean work at maintaining intellectual compatibility in the process.

It takes two to make a marriage or break a marriage, and it takes two to have an affair. The fact that he has always been a flirt suggests that, at one time, he was that way with you. You probably responded in a way that made him feel special, wanted, and needed and reinforced his flirting behavior.

This ties in with the first and main reason why men have affairs: to feed their ego. The problem with us males is that feeling good about ourselves or meeting our ego needs is our primary goal in life. Therefore, the first reason why men get involved in affairs is that it feeds their egos.

The second reason is what we call misplaced anger. For example, let's consider the husband who is extremely angry with his wife for whatever reason. He may have an affair with some other woman as a way of making his wife pay. Instead of directing his anger toward her, which he may be afraid to do, or expressing the anger in a way that will help the relationship change, he just has sex with some other woman. This action feeds his ego because someone else wants him, so he feels good physically and emotionally. And he doesn't feel as angry with his wife. In his anger, he made her pay.

The third reason why men have affairs is boredom. Proverbs 9:1 7 says, **"Stolen melons are the sweetest, stolen apples taste the best."** In modern times, the grass is greener on the other side of the fence. If I don't have enough excitement, I will create some.

Children who are raised in alcoholic homes, for example, become what we refer to as "adult children of alcoholics." One key characteristic is that they become easily bored with life should it become too stable. Children in alcoholic homes are raised with no stability. As adults, they are then more comfortable in an unstable environment than in a stable one. This is why they become bored and create chaos, which is what is most familiar or comfortable to them. We all tend to repeat our past, whether that is a positive past or a negative past. If it was unstable then, we feel most comfortable in creating an unstable one now.

The fourth reason why men have affairs is to escape emotional pain. Our sex drive is the second strongest drive within us, second only to self-preservation. Sex, therefore, can easily be used as a strong distraction from some emotional pain we do not want to feel. Few things in life are more intense than fulfilling this sex drive with a climax or orgasm. For this reason, a man can use sex to distract himself from emotional pain, like problems at home or work. It feels good to him physically, and he gets a vacation from the rest of his feelings of hurt and pain. This is why pornography is a multi-billion-dollar industry. He can receive instant gratification just by looking at a magazine, the Internet, or a video and have a secondary benefit of taking a vacation from some internalized emotional pain.

The fifth reason is the desire for nurture and intimacy. A recent study from Florida State University found that premature babies who were massaged by their mothers on a regular daily basis developed physically 60% faster than those who did not receive this extra "touching." We all need a human touch. It is a special form of nurturing. When men don't feel nurtured and cared for by their wives, they will seek it elsewhere. Everyone (males and females) needs to be nurtured with touch.

In a nutshell, these are five reasons why men cheat on their wives.

1. LOSS OF EGO A man's primary need is to feel good about himself. When he doesn't, he finds ways to meet this primary goal.

2. MISPLACED ANGER He may be angry at his wife, but rather than deal with the problem, he has an affair to make her pay.

3. **BOREDOM** Affairs are rarely boring; they are exciting and full of life. Even the fear of getting caught causes excitement.

4. **ESCAPE FROM EMOTIONAL PAIN** The male sex drive provides a distraction or vacation from emotional pain.

5. **NEED FOR NURTURING AND INTIMACY** If these needs are being met, men do not need to look elsewhere.

Many men cheat because they can. So many men cheat because they think it's exciting, different, and fun. They also cheat because the marriage that they're in right now is boring and dull. Though it may sound clichéd, any wife who starts communicating with her husband will find the best way of winning him back. She needs to impress upon him that cheating is simple; a relationship is more complex. Cheating usually offers instant gratification, physically and emotionally. A relationship requires maintenance. Giving it care and attention, along with trust and communication, will continuously help both of you grow.

Ten Ways to Know a Man Is Cheating on His Wife

1. You're suspicious. If you generically suspect every man you meet of this, it's a prejudice and not worth much. However, if you suddenly get suspicious about the individual man you're dealing with, then trust your instincts. Where there's smoke, there's fire.

2. His tone of voice gets guarded, or he won't make eye contact, and is evasive when

certain topics come up, like family, children, vacations, where he lives, etc.

3. He insists that all contact is on his terms only. He explains why you must only call him at work or on his cell. Disregard the reason. They can be ingenious about this, and if you're love-daffy, you'll find a way to rationalize his particular excuse. Don't.

4. You ask for his home phone number, and he refuses to give it to you. Again, disregard the reason.

5. His heart is not on the line. You sense an imbalance of vulnerability, and this is intuitive. When two available people are dating, both presumably are anxious for it to work out and are equally at risk. When you're playing for keeps, and

he's just playing, he won't care as much about how you're getting along. He has the security of the marriage and nothing to lose but an exciting, good time.

6. There's a white line on the fourth finger of his left hand, a tan line from where his wedding ring usually is and is not when he's with you. Or there's the outline of a ring in his shirt pocket.

7. He isn't fully disclosing when it would seem appropriate. He alludes to things he'll tell you about later.

8. He gives strange reasons for not wanting to go to certain places (like your favorite restaurant). You first met him at a dance hall (where he's known, and someone might tell his

wife). After that, every place he takes you to is in another country. (There's a part of town he definitely avoids. Guess why?)

9. He seems strangely addicted to paying for restaurants, motels, resorts, and airplane tickets in cash rather than by credit card.

10. He is never available on Sundays. In some cultures, and with many men,

Saturday night may be a 'boys' night out,' but Sunday is strictly family

time. Ditto for holidays. This is part of that peculiar male honor code:

It's OK to cheat, but not on July 4th. That's family time.

Principles of Manhood

Principles of Manhood

Chapter Five

"But without faith it is impossible to please him: for he that cometh to God must believe that he is, and that he is a rewarder of them that diligently seek him."
Hebrews 11:6 (KJV)

What God Will Do When a Man is Faithful

God will give you the desires of your heart! God wants us to enjoy everything that our world has to offer. When God created this world, He had you and me in his mind, and everything that he spoke into existence was made so that we would enjoy it with each other. God wants us to enjoy our lives as we live every day, 24 hours a day, seven days a week. Solomon said,

"Behold that which I have seen: it is good and comely for one to eat and to drink, and to enjoy the good of all his labor that he taketh under the sun all the days of his life, which God giveth him: for it is his portion. Every man also

to whom God hath given riches and wealth, and hath given him power to eat thereof, and to take his portion, and to rejoice in his labour; this is the gift of God" Ecclesiastes 5:17, 18 (KJV).

Many things in life will bring you money, status, power, and influence. Your achievements and successes will bring great possessions and put you before great people, but never forfeit your relationship with God. There is a spiritual prosperity that God wants to manifest in our lives. God wants us to be enriched bountifully with his wisdom. God wants every man to be filled with the knowledge of His will. He wants us to have wisdom and spiritual understanding. Paul said,

"For this cause, we also, since the day we heard it, do not cease to pray for you, and to desire that ye might be filled with the

knowledge of his will in all wisdom and spiritual understanding; That ye might walk worthy of the Lord unto all pleasing, being fruitful in every good work, and increasing in the knowledge of God" Colossians 1:9, 10 (KJV).

When facing a problem that requires a wise decision, a man does not need prosperity in the form of money; you need wisdom from God. You need a word of knowledge. As we strive to reach a point where we are increasing materially, we need to strive to increase in the knowledge and wisdom of God. If we are filled with the knowledge of His will, then we know that He wants us to prosper in whatever we undertake. There is no pleasure, power, influence, or connection, like being connected with God. Our Lord and Savior said,

"Consider the lilies how they grow: they toil not, they spin not; and yet I say unto you, that Solomon in all his glory was not arrayed like one of these. If then God so clothe the grass, which is today in the field, and to morrow is cast into the oven; how much more will he clothe you, O ye of little faith? And seek not ye what ye shall eat, or what ye shall drink, neither be ye of doubtful mind. For all these things do the world's nations seek after: and your Father knoweth that ye need these things. But rather seek ye the kingdom of God; and all these things shall be added unto you" Luke 12:27-31 (KJV).

All our achievements and possessions are good in their place, but we must remember that they tend to make us think they're the source of happiness. They make us feel good, but they don't bring true happiness. They do not bring contentment. Paul, writing to the Philippians church about being content, said,

"Finally, brethren, whatsoever things are true, whatsoever things are honest, whatsoever things are just, whatsoever things are pure, whatsoever things are lovely, whatsoever things are of good report; if there be any virtue, and if there be any praise, think on these things. Those things, which ye have both learned, and received, and heard, and seen in me, do: and the God of peace shall be with you. But I rejoiced in the Lord greatly, that now at the last your care of me hath flourished again; wherein ye were also careful, but ye lacked opportunity. Not that I speak in respect of want: for I have learned, in whatsoever state I am, therewith to be content. I know both how to be abased, and I know how to abound: everywhere

and in all things, I am instructed both to be full and to be hungry, both to abound and to suffer need. I can do all things through Christ which strengtheneth me" Philippians 4:8-13 (KJV).

God wants us to enjoy these things, but enjoying these things is not the reason God put us here. God has created us with a purpose. The Bible is summed up with two commands: love God and love your neighbor, and Paul sums up the whole law with the statement: love your neighbor. So, God's purpose for us is to love others, to build relationships, to move into other people's lives, and to help them move towards God. We will find the most joy in life when building relationships... so, we must align our motives to building relationships.

Yes, the one element that truly makes a man faithful is when his motives are clearly defined. Don't ask just to be blessed for your own personal gain. Ask to be blessed so that you may bring souls to the church and, ultimately, into the Kingdom of God. Ask to be blessed so that all you do helps others. You should always want to feed the hungry, clothe the naked, and educate the illiterate. Always be aware of blessing God's Kingdom with your giving. When you sincerely do all you can to become an avenue for God's prosperity, God will entrust you with the true riches of His Kingdom.

Each of us will be rewarded for the seeds that we sow. However, be sure to operate with a true and sincere heart, not out of a spirit of greed but motivated by a spirit of building relationships with family, friends, and associates. Our faith and relationship with God should reach a point where we continue to serve whether we have or have not. Whether we're blessed from tithing, or we're not, we must continue to tithe. We must remain faithful in giving regardless of whether we receive something in return.

This is the type of relationship we should pursue with God. When our priorities and relationship with God are in order, God will bless us even when we don't ask Him to bless us.

Everything in this world belongs to God. Your house, your car, and your job belong to God. Your boss at work may think he can determine your salary, but he does not determine your income. God will add to your salary and prosper you in ways you never imagined. You may look to your boss for your salary, but you must look to God for your income. You may be making minimum wage, but God will bless you in all avenues. Just continue to be faithful, coming in and going out. Your income from God will far exceed your salary.

When your needs are met, what more can you ask God for? But God is so faithful that he will give you the desires of your heart. What desires do you harbor in your heart? Be faithful, and true prosperity will be your running buddy. Paul said he knew how to abase and how to abound; he knew how to be content when he was hungry and how to be content when he was full. He learned how to be prosperous in all that he undertook. He knew how to get along when things were scarce and when things were plenteous. A faithful man of God will experience true prosperity and true blessings when he has a faithful relationship with God.

Principles of Manhood

About the Author

Edward N. Jackson was born in Nashville, Tennessee, March 11, 1951. His college years were spent at Tennessee State University (TSU), where he received his BS in Technical Aeronautics and his Commission as 2nd Lieutenant and pilot, in the United States Air Force. Presently, Ed is concerned with helping others to have the mindset to master life, serving as a mindset coach, facilitator and motivational speaker who specializes in financial matters as he launches his mindset business, "Genesis."

www.ingramcontent.com/pod-product-compliance
Lightning Source LLC
Chambersburg PA
CBHW071227160426
43196CB00012B/2433